1911 OHIO DOMINICAN COLLEGE

LIBRARY

1216 SUNBURY RD.
COLUMBUS, OHIO

Donated By:
Martha Galoway
Petrucci   '56

Gift of

Count on Leo Lion

By Donna Pape

Drawings by Tom Eaton

GARRARD PUBLISHING COMPANY
CHAMPAIGN, ILLINOIS

Copyright © 1973 by Donna Lugg Pape   All rights reserved. Manufactured in the U.S.A.
International Standard Book Number: 8116–6724–3   Library of Congress Catalog Card Number: 72–9093

Count on Leo Lion

Leo Lion was sleeping.
But soon he woke up.
Two monkeys
in the next cage
were shouting.

"You ate more peanuts
than I did,"
one monkey said.
"I did not,"
said the other monkey.
Leo opened the door
of his cage.

He walked
to the monkey cage.
"Stop that noise!"
Leo said.
"I want to sleep.
You should count
your peanuts."

One monkey jumped
on a swing.
"Count?" he asked.
"What is that?"

"I know how to count,"
said the other monkey.
He counted:
"1, 10, 7, 3, 6, 5."

"That's not right,"
Leo said.
"I'll teach you
how to count."
"We want to learn,"
they said.
"I'll count my steps,"
Leo said.
He walked and counted:
"1, 2, 3, 4, 5,
6, 7, 8, 9, 10."
The monkeys said,
"You walk too fast.
We can't count your steps."

Then Leo walked
and counted more slowly.
"We can't remember
how to count slow steps,"
the monkeys said.

Leo opened the door
of the monkeys' cage.
"Come on," he said.
"Let's find something
easy to count."

They walked
around the zoo.
They stopped
by many cages.
Leo looked
at all the animals.

MALAYAN TAPIR

The animals looked
at Leo and the monkeys.
"It will be hard
to count animals," Leo said.
"We'll have to find
something else to count."

Finally they came
to the bird cage.
"There are too many birds
to count," Leo said.

Beside the bird cage
Leo picked up ten feathers.
He took them back
to the monkeys' cage.
Leo put the feathers
in a row.

He put his paw
on one feather.
"This is one feather,"
he said.
"One feather,"
said the monkeys.

Just then
the other nine feathers
blew away.
"It's too hard
to count feathers,"
Leo said.

Leo led the monkeys
out of the zoo.
"We'll count people,"
Leo said.

A bus was coming
down the street.
It stopped by them.

"We'll count the people
on this bus," Leo said.
Leo and the monkeys
got on the bus.

"Help! Help!"
the people shouted.
All of them
ran out the back door.
Leo and the monkeys
got off too.

"We'll have to find
something else to count,"
Leo said.
He saw a man
with some balloons.
"We'll count balloons,"
Leo said.

He and the monkeys
went up to the man.
The man turned around.
When he saw Leo,
he let go
of his balloons.
He ran down the street.

The balloons
went up, up
into the sky.
"We can't count balloons,"
Leo said to the monkeys.

"Besides, I'm getting hungry.
It must be time to eat.
Let's go back
to the zoo."

Leo and the monkeys
went back to their cages.
Soon the monkeys
started to fight again.
"I must find a way
to teach those monkeys
how to count,"
Leo said.
Just then
a little girl
who was jumping rope
came by Leo's cage.
She looked at Leo
and began to sing:

1 lion
feels his nose.

2 lions
smell a rose.

3 lions
lie on the floor.

4 lions
look out the door.

5 lions
try to sing.

6 lions
make a ring.

7 lions
watch a show.

8 lions
stand in a row.

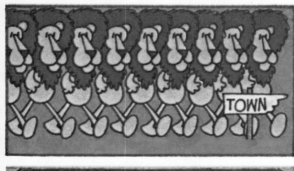

9 lions
go to town.

10 lions
jump up and down.

Leo was pleased.

He called to the monkeys,

"I will sing

that song for you.

Then you can count
your peanuts."
Leo sang the song
over and over.

The monkeys listened.
Soon they were singing too.
"Now they can count
their peanuts," Leo said.

"They'll be quiet
and I can sleep."
Leo smiled.
He lay down
for a nice long nap.

But soon the monkeys
were fighting again.
"I taught you
how to count," said Leo.

"Why don't you count
your peanuts?"
"We don't know
how to count peanuts,"
they said.
"We can only count lions."
Leo laughed.
"If you can count lions,
you can count anything,"
he said.
"But I will make up
a peanut song for you."
Leo thought
and then he sang:

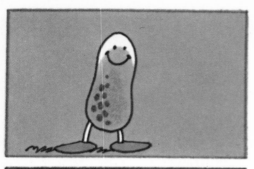

1 peanut
has a face.

2 peanuts
have a race.

3 peanuts
sit in a bowl.

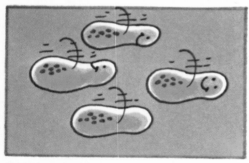

4 peanuts
start to roll.

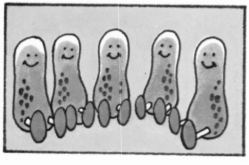

5 peanuts
are on the ground.

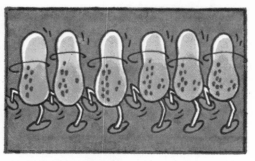

6 peanuts
turn around.

7 peanuts
hide in a bag.

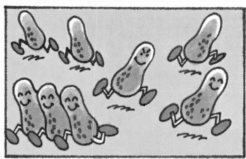

8 peanuts
are playing tag.

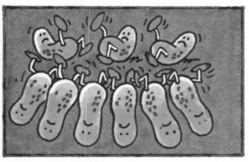

9 peanuts
try to stand.

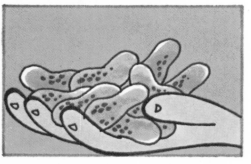

10 peanuts
now lie
in a monkey's hand.

Again and again Leo sang.
Soon the monkeys
could sing the song.
Leo watched them
count their peanuts.
Each monkey got ten.

Then Leo Lion
closed his eyes
and fell asleep.
He had a big smile
on his face.